Contents

Python... for your project?

Python... for your project?

Introduction

In recent years, Python has emerged as one of the most popular programming languages for software development. With its simplicity, flexibility, and extensive library support, Python has become a go-to language for a wide range of applications, from web development and data science to machine learning and artificial intelligence. In this book, we'll take a closer look at the latest trends and developments in Python coding and software development and explore how these trends are shaping the future of the industry.

Chapter 1:

Python's Growing Popularity

"A look at the latest trends and developments in Python coding and software development and how these trends are shaping the future of the industry."

Python has been on the rise as a dominant language in software development for several years. There are several reasons why Python has become so popular:

Ease of use and readability: Python has a simple and easy-to-learn syntax, which makes it accessible to programmers of all levels. Its readability also makes it easier to maintain and debug code, which saves time and resources.

Versatility: Python is a general-purpose language, which means it can be used for a wide range of applications, from web development to scientific computing. It also has a vast standard library and many third-party packages that provide additional functionality.

Data science and machine learning: Python has become the go-to language for data science and machine learning due to its powerful libraries such as NumPy, Pandas, and TensorFlow. This has driven its adoption in many industries that rely on data analysis and artificial intelligence.

Community support: Python has a large and active community of developers, which has led to the creation of numerous resources, including libraries, frameworks, and tools. This support has made it easier to learn and use Python and has also contributed to its growth in popularity.

Industry adoption: Many companies, including tech giants like Google, Facebook, and Amazon, have adopted Python for various purposes, from web development to data analysis and machine learning. This has led to increased demand for Python skills among developers and has driven its rise as a dominant language in software development.

Overall, Python's ease of use, versatility, powerful libraries for data science and machine learning, community support, and industry adoption have all contributed to its rise as a dominant language in software development. As these trends continue, Python will likely remain a popular and important language in the years to come.

The reasons behind Python's popularity.

Python's popularity can be attributed to several factors, including its ease of use, flexibility, and broad library support. Here are some more details on each of these factors:

Ease of use: Python has a simple syntax that is easy to learn, read, and write. It has a relatively small number of keywords and built-in functions, which makes it less complex than other programming languages like C++ or Java. This simplicity makes it accessible to both novice and experienced programmers and enables faster prototyping and development.

Flexibility: Python is a general-purpose language that can be used for a wide variety of tasks, including web development, scientific computing, data analysis, and automation. Its versatility is due to its dynamic nature, which allows it to be used for scripting, as well as for larger software projects.

Broad library support: Python has a vast library of third-party packages that extend its functionality and make it easier to write complex programmes. These libraries cover a range of domains, including web development, data science, machine learning, and natural language processing. The most popular libraries include NumPy, Pandas, Scikit-Learn, TensorFlow, and Django, among others.

Community support: Python has a large and active community of developers, which has contributed to its popularity and growth. The community provides a wealth of resources, including documentation, tutorials, forums, and code snippets, which makes it easier to learn and use Python. This support also results in the rapid development of new libraries and frameworks.

Industry adoption: Python has been adopted by many industries, including tech giants like Google, Facebook, and Amazon, which have integrated Python into their products and services. Python's popularity in data science and machine learning has also contributed to its adoption in the finance, healthcare, and automotive industries.

In summary, Python's popularity is driven by its ease of use, flexibility, broad library support, strong community, and industry adoption. These factors have led to a virtuous cycle where more developers use Python, which leads to the development of more libraries and tools, further increasing its popularity. As a result, Python has become one of the most widely used and versatile programming languages today.

The Impact of Python's Popularity on the software development industry

Python's popularity has had a significant impact on the software development industry, affecting the way companies approach software development, hiring, and innovation. Here are some of the key ways Python's popularity has impacted the software development industry:

Increased productivity: Python's ease of use, simplicity, and extensive library support have led to increased productivity among software developers. With Python, developers can write code faster, prototype applications quickly, and spend less time debugging and maintaining code. This increased productivity has enabled companies to deliver software products faster and more efficiently, reducing time-to-market and costs.

Growing demand for Python developers: The rise of Python's popularity has resulted in a growing demand for developers who are proficient in the language. As more companies adopt Python, the need for skilled Python developers has increased, leading to higher salaries and more opportunities for those who specialise in the language. This has also led to more training programmes and courses to help developers learn Python. There is also a growing demand seen at recruitment companies to supply software development candidates with knowledge and experience of Python.

Increased innovation: Python's versatility and broad library support have encouraged innovation in the software development industry. With Python, developers can quickly and easily create new applications and experiment with new technologies. This has led to the development of new tools and frameworks, such as NumPy, Pandas, and Django, which have transformed data science, web development, and automation.

Enhanced data science capabilities: Python's popularity in data science has transformed the industry's approach to data analysis, visualisation, and machine learning. The language's extensive library support for data science, including NumPy, Pandas, and Scikit-learn, has made it easier to work with large datasets and develop complex models. This has led to breakthroughs in fields such as healthcare, finance, and engineering.

Adoption by tech giants: Python's popularity has led to its adoption by tech giants such as Google, Facebook, and Amazon, which use the language to develop their products and services. This has helped to drive Python's popularity further and provided a wealth of resources, such as open-source libraries, tools, and training, for developers to learn from.

In summary, Python's popularity has transformed the software development industry, enabling faster development, increasing productivity, and driving innovation. The language's versatility, broad library support, and ease of use have made it a go-to language for many software development projects, from data science and automation to web development and machine learning. The impact of Python's popularity is likely to continue to shape the industry in the years to come.

Chapter 2:

Advances in Python Development Tools

"Lets explore the latest advances in Python development tools, including IDEs, frameworks, and libraries".

Python's popularity has spurred a wealth of development tools, frameworks, and libraries that have made it easier and more efficient to develop Python applications. Here are some of the latest advances in Python development tools:

Integrated Development Environments (IDEs): IDEs provide an integrated development environment that combines a code editor with debugging tools, code completion, and other features. Some of the most popular Python IDEs include PyCharm, VS Code, and Spyder. These IDEs provide features such as intelligent code completion, debugging, and code profiling to make it easier to develop and maintain Python code.

Web Frameworks: Python has several popular web frameworks that make it easier to develop web applications. These frameworks provide a set of tools and libraries to simplify tasks such as routing, authentication, and database integration. Some of the most popular Python web frameworks include Django, Flask, and Pyramid.

Libraries: Python has a vast ecosystem of libraries that provide developers with tools for tasks such as data analysis, machine learning, and automation. Some of the most popular Python libraries include NumPy, Pandas, Matplotlib, and Scikit-learn. These libraries provide developers with a set of pre-built functions and tools that make it easier to perform complex tasks.

Code Editors: Code editors provide a lightweight alternative to IDEs, providing developers with a basic set of features for editing and running Python code. Some of the most popular Python code editors include Sublime Text, Atom, and Visual Studio Code. These editors provide syntax highlighting, code completion, and other features that make it easier to write Python code.

Testing Frameworks: Testing frameworks provide developers with tools for testing Python code. Some of the most popular testing frameworks include PyTest, unittest, and doctest. These frameworks provide developers with a set of tools for writing tests and ensuring that their code is functioning correctly.

Debugging Tools: Debugging tools provide developers with tools for debugging Python code. Some of the most popular Python debugging tools include PyCharm Debugger, pdb, and IPython Debugger. These tools provide developers with a set of tools for finding and fixing bugs in their code.

In summary, Python has a vast ecosystem of development tools, frameworks, and libraries that make it easier and more efficient to develop Python applications. These tools provide developers with a set of pre-built functions and tools that make it easier to perform complex tasks, such as data analysis, machine learning, and web development. As Python's popularity continues to grow, we can expect to see further advances in the development tools available to Python developers.

The benefits of using Python Development Tools and how they can improve productivity and efficiency

Using development tools for software development provides several benefits, including increased productivity and efficiency. Here are some ways that development tools can improve the software development process:

Faster Development: Development tools such as integrated development environments (IDEs) and code editors provide features such as syntax highlighting, code completion, and code formatting, which can speed up development time. These tools can also provide templates and wizards for common tasks, reducing the time required to complete repetitive tasks.

Improved Code Quality: Development tools such as testing frameworks and debugging tools can help ensure that code is written correctly and performs as expected. Testing frameworks allow developers to write tests that automatically verify that code works as intended while debugging tools help identify and fix errors in code.

Simplified Collaboration: Development tools can simplify collaboration between team members by providing version control and collaboration features. Version control tools such as Git allow teams to work on code simultaneously without overwriting each other's work. Collaboration features such as code reviews and comments can also improve communication between team members.

Easy Maintenance: Development tools can make it easier to maintain code by providing features such as refactoring and code analysis. Refactoring tools allow developers to restructure code without changing its behaviour, while code analysis tools can identify potential errors or performance issues.

Increased Efficiency: Development tools can increase efficiency by automating repetitive tasks and providing shortcuts and templates for common tasks. This can save time and reduce errors, allowing developers to focus on more complex tasks.

Overall, using development tools can improve productivity and efficiency in software development by speeding up development time, improving code quality, simplifying collaboration, facilitating maintenance, and increasing efficiency. As the number of available development tools continues to grow, developers can expect to benefit from more sophisticated and specialized tools for their specific needs.

Examples of popular Python development tools and their use-cases.

Python has a large and active development community, which has resulted in many popular and powerful development tools. Here are some examples of popular Python development tools and their use cases:

Integrated Development Environments (IDEs): IDEs are comprehensive development environments that integrate all the tools needed for software development. Some popular Python IDEs include PyCharm, Spyder, and Visual Studio Code. PyCharm is an IDE that provides features such as code completion, debugging, and testing. Spyder is a scientific IDE that is used for data analysis and scientific computing. Visual Studio Code is a lightweight, cross-platform IDE that provides support for Python through extensions. Real-life examples of companies using PyCharm include Dropbox and Netflix.

Web Frameworks: Python has many powerful web frameworks, including Django, Flask, and Pyramid. Django is a full-stack web framework that provides an ORM, templating engine, and a robust admin interface. Flask is a lightweight framework that is easy to set up and provides the basic features needed for web development. Pyramid is a flexible and scalable web framework that provides support for both small and large projects. Real-life examples of companies using Django include Instagram and Mozilla.

Data Analysis Tools: Python has many powerful data analysis libraries, including NumPy, Pandas, and SciPy. NumPy is a library for numerical computing that provides support for large arrays and matrices. Pandas is a library for data manipulation that provides support for data analysis and visualization. SciPy is a library for scientific computing that provides support for optimization, integration, and linear algebra. Real-life examples of companies using Pandas include JP Morgan and Amazon.

Machine Learning Tools: Python has become the de facto language for machine learning and has many powerful libraries, including TensorFlow, Keras, and PyTorch. TensorFlow is an open-source machine learning framework that provides support for deep learning and neural networks. Keras is a high-level library that provides an API for building and training neural networks. PyTorch is a machine-learning library that provides support for dynamic computation graphs. Real-life examples of companies using TensorFlow include Airbnb and Uber.

Testing Tools: Python has many powerful testing libraries, including pytest, unittest, and doctest. Pytest is a testing framework that provides support for test discovery, fixtures, and plugins. Unittest is a testing framework that provides support for test automation, fixtures, and assertions. Doctest is a testing framework that allows developers to write tests in the form of code examples. Real-life examples of companies using pytest include Dropbox and Mozilla.

In summary, Python has a rich ecosystem of development tools that cater to a wide range of use cases. From web frameworks to data analysis tools to machine learning libraries, Python's versatility and ease of use make it an attractive choice for developers. Real-life examples of companies using Python and its development tools span a wide range of industries, from technology to finance to entertainment.

Chapter 3

Python in Data Science and Machine Learning

Python is widely used in the field of data science and machine learning due to several advantages it offers over other programming languages.

Firstly, Python has a rich and powerful library ecosystem specifically designed for data science and machine learning tasks. Some popular libraries include NumPy, Pandas, Matplotlib, and Scikit-learn. These libraries provide pre-built functions and algorithms for various tasks such as data analysis, visualization, and modelling, which significantly speeds up the development process.

Secondly, Python has a simple and easy-to-understand syntax, which makes it more accessible to beginners compared to other programming languages. This ease of use allows data scientists to focus on the analysis and modelling tasks, rather than getting bogged down in the technical details of the programming language.

Thirdly, Python has strong community support, which is continuously developing new libraries and tools to meet the demands of the field. This makes it easier for data scientists to stay up-to-date with the latest advancements and integrate them into their projects.

Python is also highly compatible with popular machine learning frameworks such as TensorFlow, Keras, and PyTorch. These frameworks provide pre-built functions and tools for building and training machine learning models, making the process more efficient and streamlined.

Overall, Python's advantages in data science and machine learning have led to its widespread adoption in the field and have contributed to its continued growth and popularity.

Key Python libraries and frameworks for data science and machine learning.

Python has a rich and powerful library ecosystem specifically designed for data science and machine learning tasks. Some of the key libraries and frameworks for data science and machine learning in Python include:

NumPy: NumPy is a fundamental library for scientific computing in Python. It provides support for multidimensional arrays, complex mathematical functions, and random number generators. NumPy is a fundamental building block for many other Python libraries and frameworks, including Pandas, Matplotlib, and Scikit-learn.

Pandas: Pandas is a powerful library for data manipulation and analysis in Python. It provides data structures for efficiently handling large datasets, including DataFrame and Series objects.

Pandas provides support for data cleaning, filtering, aggregation, and other data manipulation tasks.

Matplotlib: Matplotlib is a popular visualization library in Python. It provides support for creating a wide range of static, animated, and interactive plots, charts, and diagrams. Matplotlib is highly customizable and provides support for creating publication-quality graphics.

Scikit-learn: Scikit-learn is a popular machine-learning library in Python. It provides support for many common machine-learning tasks, including classification, regression, clustering, and dimensionality reduction. Scikit-learn also provides support for model evaluation and validation.

TensorFlow: TensorFlow is an open-source machine learning framework in Python. It provides support for building and training neural networks, deep learning models, and other machine learning models. TensorFlow is highly scalable and provides support for distributed computing.

These libraries and frameworks provide pre-built functions and algorithms for various tasks such as data analysis, visualization, and modeling, which significantly speeds up the development process. They are widely used in the data science and machine learning communities and have contributed to Python's popularity and growth in these fields.

Case studies of successful data science and machine learning projects using Python

Here are three in-depth case studies of successful data science and machine learning projects that used Python:

Case study 1: Predictive maintenance at ThyssenKrupp

ThyssenKrupp, a German multinational conglomerate, used data science and machine learning to predict when their elevators will require maintenance. They developed a predictive maintenance system using Python and machine learning algorithms that analyse data from sensors installed in the elevators. The system helped reduce downtime and maintenance costs and improve overall elevator reliability.

Case Study 2: Spotify's music recommendation engine

Spotify uses machine learning to provide personalised music recommendations to its users. They developed a music recommendation engine that uses Python and machine learning algorithms to analyse user data, such as listening history, and suggest songs and playlists that are likely to be of interest. The engine takes several factors into account, including genre, artist, and popularity, to provide relevant recommendations. The system has been highly successful, contributing to Spotify's growth and user engagement.

Case Study 3: Autonomous Driving at Waymo

Waymo, a subsidiary of Alphabet Inc., is a leading developer of autonomous driving technology. They used Python and machine learning to develop their self-driving cars' perception systems, which enable the vehicles to detect and interpret their surroundings. They used a deep learning algorithm called convolutional neural networks (CNNs) to process data from sensors, such as cameras and lidar, and identify objects and obstacles on the road. The system has been highly successful, with Waymo's autonomous vehicles having driven millions of miles on public roads.

These three case studies described above, demonstrate the power and versatility of Python in developing data science and machine learning applications in various industries. Python's rich library ecosystem, combined with its ease of use and flexibility, has made it a popular choice for data science and machine learning projects.

Chapter 4

Python in Web Development

"Understand the use of Python in web development, and its advantages".

Python has become increasingly popular for web development, particularly for building complex and large-scale web applications. Here are some advantages of using Python over other languages like PHP and JavaScript:

Clean and readable syntax: Python has a simple and clean syntax that is easy to read and understand, making it easier to write and maintain code. This can improve development speed and reduce errors.

Large and robust library ecosystem: Python has a vast library ecosystem that includes many useful modules and frameworks for web development. This can save development time and effort, as developers don't need to reinvent the wheel for common tasks.

Scalability: Python is well-suited for building large and complex web applications that need to scale. Python's multi-threading and multi-processing capabilities make it possible to handle heavy loads and high traffic volumes.

Cross-platform compatibility: Python code can run on any platform that supports it, making it easy to develop and deploy web applications across multiple operating systems.

Versatility: Python can be used for a variety of web development tasks, from server-side scripting to database management and front-end development. This makes it a versatile language that can be used for a wide range of projects.

While languages like PHP and JavaScript are also popular for web development, Python's advantages make it a compelling choice for developers looking for a flexible and powerful language to build their web applications with.

Popular Python web development frameworks

Python has several popular web development frameworks that make it easier to build web applications. Here are some of the most commonly used frameworks:

Django: Django is a high-level Python web framework that emphasizes rapid development and clean, pragmatic design. It includes many built-in features like a powerful ORM, automatic admin interface, and routing system, making it easy to build complex web applications quickly.

Flask: Flask is a lightweight and flexible Python web framework that is great for building small to medium-sized web applications. It is easy to learn and use and includes many useful extensions that make it easy to add features like authentication and database support.

Pyramid: Pyramid is a general-purpose Python web framework that emphasizes flexibility and scalability. It includes many built-in features like a powerful routing system, a templating engine, and database support, making it a good choice for building large and complex web applications.

Bottle: Bottle is a fast and simple Python web framework that is great for building small web applications or APIs. It is easy to learn and use and includes many useful features like a built-in templating engine and support for various database backends.

CherryPy: CherryPy is a minimalist Python web framework that emphasises simplicity and ease of use. It includes many built-in features, like a powerful routing system, a built-in web server, and support for various database backends.

Each of these frameworks has its strengths and weaknesses, and the choice of which one to use depends on the specific requirements of the project. However, Django and Flask are currently the most popular Python web frameworks, thanks to their ease of use, a wide range of features, and large and active developer communities.

Examples of successful web development projects using Python

Dropbox: Dropbox is a cloud-based file storage and sharing service that uses Python as its main programming language. Python is used extensively in the backend to handle tasks like file syncing, metadata indexing, and file encryption.

Instagram: Instagram is a popular photo and video-sharing social networking platform that uses Python in its backend to handle tasks like serving images and videos, processing data feeds, and managing the content database.

SurveyMonkey: SurveyMonkey is a web-based survey platform that uses Python as its main programming language. Python is used in the backend to handle tasks like survey creation, data analysis, and report generation.

Pinterest: Pinterest is a social media platform that allows users to discover, save, and share images and videos. Python is used extensively in the backend to handle tasks like image processing, content delivery, and machine learning-based recommendation algorithms.

Reddit: Reddit is a social news aggregation and discussion platform that uses Python in its backend to handle tasks like content moderation, user authentication, and content recommendation.

All of these projects showcase the flexibility and power of Python as a web development language and highlight its ability to handle a wide range of tasks and applications.

Chapter 5

Which is better...PHP, JavaScript or Python?

*"Before you decide, weigh up the pro's and cons.
What are the benefits?"*

What are the benefits of using Python over PHP and JavaScript? Python, PHP, and JavaScript are all popular programming languages used in web development, and each has its strengths and weaknesses. Here are a few benefits of using Python over PHP and JavaScript:

Ease of Use: Python is known for its simple and intuitive syntax, making it easier to read and write code compared to PHP and JavaScript. Python code tends to be more concise and expressive, which can save time and reduce the potential for errors.

Flexibility: Python is a versatile language that can be used for a wide range of applications, from web development and data science to machine learning and artificial intelligence. This flexibility allows developers to use Python across multiple projects and industries, making it a valuable language to learn.

Large Library Support: Python has a large and growing collection of libraries and frameworks that can be used for web development and other applications. These libraries make it easy to build complex applications quickly and efficiently, reducing the amount of time and effort required to build software.

Strong Community Support: Python has a large and active community of developers who contribute to the language and its libraries. This community support means that there are plenty of resources available for learning Python and troubleshooting problems, making it easier for developers to get started with the language.

Of course, the choice of programming language depends on the specific needs of each project and the preferences of the development team. Python may not always be the best choice for every application, and there are certainly benefits to using PHP and JavaScript as well. However, for many developers and businesses, Python's ease of use, flexibility, library support, and community make it a compelling choice for web development and beyond.

Why would JavaScript be more suitable than Python?

JavaScript and Python are both powerful programming languages, but they have different strengths and weaknesses that make them more or less suitable for certain types of projects. Here are a few reasons why JavaScript might be more suitable than Python for certain applications:

Client-Side Web Development: JavaScript is the primary language used for client-side web development, allowing developers to create interactive and dynamic web pages that respond to user input. While Python can be used for web development, it is generally better suited for server-side programming.

Cross-Platform Compatibility: JavaScript is a language that runs on all major web browsers and operating systems, making it a good choice for developing cross-platform applications. Python, on the other hand, requires a separate runtime environment to be installed on each system, which can make deployment more complex.

Speed: JavaScript is typically faster than Python for certain types of applications, such as those that involve real-time updates or high levels of interactivity. This is because JavaScript is a client-side language that runs in the browser, while Python typically runs on the server side.

Popularity and Community: JavaScript is one of the most widely-used programming languages in the world, with a large and active community of developers who contribute to its development and support. This popularity and community support make it easier to find resources and tools for JavaScript development, which can be a major advantage for some projects.

Of course, the choice of programming language ultimately depends on the specific requirements of the project and the preferences and expertise of the development team. While JavaScript may be more suitable for certain applications, Python is a powerful language with many advantages of its own and can be a good choice for many types of projects.

Why would JavaScript be better than PHP?

JavaScript and PHP are both popular programming languages used in web development, but they have different strengths and weaknesses that make them more or less suitable for certain types of projects. Here are a few reasons why JavaScript might be better than PHP for certain applications:

Client-Side Web Development: JavaScript is the primary language used for client-side web development, allowing developers to create interactive and dynamic web pages that respond to user input. PHP, on the other hand, is typically used for server-side programming, which is responsible for generating the HTML that is sent to the browser.

Asynchronous Programming: JavaScript is well-suited for asynchronous programming, which allows developers to write code that runs non-blocking, meaning that it does not block other code from running while it waits for a response. This is particularly useful for building real-time web applications, such as chat applications, where multiple users can interact with each other simultaneously. PHP can also be used for asynchronous programming, but it is typically less well-suited for this task than JavaScript.

Popularity and Community: JavaScript is one of the most widely-used programming languages in the world, with a large and active community of developers who contribute to its development and support. This popularity and community support make it easier to find resources and tools for JavaScript development, which can be a major advantage for some projects.

Browser Support: JavaScript is a language that runs on all major web browsers, making it an essential tool for creating interactive web applications. PHP, on the other hand, is typically used on the server side and is not directly supported by web browsers.

Of course, the choice of programming language ultimately depends on the specific requirements of the project and the preferences and expertise of the development team. While JavaScript may be better than PHP for certain applications, PHP is a powerful language with many advantages of its own and can be a good choice for many types of web development projects.

What kind of web development projects are most suited to Python, PHP, and JS?

Here are some examples of web development projects that are most suited to Python, PHP, and JavaScript:

Python:

Web applications that involve data analysis and machine learning

Scientific and numerical computing applications

Web development projects that involve a lot of text processing, such as content management systems and blogging platforms

Projects that require complex algorithms and logic, such as AI-based chatbots and recommendation systems

Large-scale web applications with high traffic volumes and complex workflows

PHP:

Server-side web applications and dynamic web pages that require access to databases and user authentication

Content management systems, such as WordPress and Drupal

E-commerce applications and online shopping carts

Web applications that require integration with payment gateways or APIs

Forums, social networks, and other community-driven websites

JavaScript:

Client-side web applications that run in the browser, such as single-page applications (SPAs)

Web applications that require real-time updates, such as chat applications and social media platforms

Interactive and dynamic web pages that respond to user input, such as games and multimedia applications Web applications that require data visualisation, such as dashboards and data analytics tools

Cross-platform mobile applications that use web technologies, such as React Native and Ionic

Of course, these are just general guidelines, and the choice of programming language ultimately depends on the specific requirements of the project and the preferences and expertise of the development team. Many web development projects can be built using a combination of different programming languages and technologies, so it's important to choose the tools that are best suited to the needs of your project.

In Summary

Python is a highly versatile and popular programming language that is well-suited for a wide range of software development tasks, including web development, data science, machine learning, and more. Python's ease of use, flexibility, and broad library support has made it one of the most popular programming languages in the world, and its impact on the software development industry is evident.

Python's popularity has led to the development of a wide range of development tools, including IDEs, frameworks, and libraries, that can improve productivity and efficiency for software development teams. Some of the most popular tools for Python development include PyCharm, Django, Flask, and NumPy, among others.

When it comes to recruiting practices, it is crucial to build a team of talented developers who are familiar with Python and its various libraries and frameworks. This will ensure that the team can take full advantage of Python's capabilities and create high-quality software applications that meet the needs of the business.

In conclusion, based on the information presented in our conversation, it is clear that Python is a highly suitable language for a variety of software development tasks. Its versatility, ease of use, and wide range of libraries and frameworks make it an excellent choice for businesses looking to develop web applications, data science solutions, machine learning algorithms, and more. With the right team of developers and the right tools, Python can help businesses achieve their software development goals and stay ahead of the competition.

Final thoughts...

Python is a powerful and versatile programming language that is increasingly becoming the language of choice for software development. By staying up-to-date on the latest trends and developments in Python coding and software development, businesses and developers can stay ahead of the curve and take advantage of Python's many benefits. Whether you're building a web application, working in data science, or developing the next generation of artificial intelligence, with the right team in place, Python is a language that can help you achieve your goals.